BASIC ARRANGING TECHNIQUES FOR THE BEGINNING ARRANGER

BASIC ARRANGING TECHNIQUES FOR THE BEGINNING ARRANGER

Volume 1
by
Dr. David W. Roe

ARPress
ILLUMINATING IDEAS,
EMPOWERING VOICES

ARPress
45 Dan Road Suite 15
Canton MA 02021

Hotline:	1(888) 821-0229
Fax:	1(508) 545-7580

Ordering Information:
Quantity sales. Special discounts are available on quantity purchases by corporations, associations, and others. For details, contact the publisher at the address above.

Printed in the United States of America.

ISBN-13:	Softcover	979-8-89676-321-5
	eBook	979-8-89676-322-2

Library of Congress Control Number: 2025902400

Table of Contents

Dedication

"Dedicated to my wife Mina"

Introduction

This text serves both as a resource booklet and a workbook for the student who is interested in arranging music for small ensembles such as woodwind, brass, string, and percussion ensembles as well as larger ensembles such as the concert band. It is assumed that the student has a basic understanding of the rudiments of music including notation, scales and key signatures, intervals, meter, and transposition. However if the student is lacking this knowledge, there are some suggestions of books in the Bibliography that may be helpful.

The author, Dr. Roe, has taught instrumental and vocal music in the secondary schools of Ontario, Canada for many years. He acknowledges the fact that many schools are not equipped with materials to teach arranging and composition to students, especially at the basic level, and also that there are very few books on the market on this subject that are within the reach of most school budgets. Dr. Roe's qualifications both as an educator and a composer/arranger enable him to know what students need to understand to become involved in the practice of arranging and composition.

Because this is a text for beginning students of arranging, only the instruments of the concert band and school orchestra are included. Instruments such as the harp, contrabassoon, English horn, and bass flute are not included. The assignments give the student the opportunity of arranging music for woodwind, brass, string and percussion ensembles as well as the concert band. There are no assignments for writing for orchestra. Also not included are the use of special effects such as the use of mutes and multiphonics, the subject of string bowings, and special string techniques such as collegno, sul ponticello, harmonics, double stops, etc. The ranges given for the instruments are those which the senior high school student is probably able to produce. The blackened notes indicate notes that are possible for more experienced instrumentalists.

Generally the larger the size of the ensemble, the larger the score. Because of the size of this book, students may have some difficulty with the concert band arrangement on pages 36 and 37. Large-size score paper is available from most music stores.

Dr. Roe plans to write a second volume about arranging which will give the student a more advanced look at the practice arranging for various ensembles including the orchestra as well as an introduction to choral arranging. If you are interested in purchasing Volume 2, you may write to Dr. David W. Roe at dwrmusicco@ gmail.com.

TRANSPOSITION OF INSTRUMENTS

1. NON-TRANSPOSING INSTRUMENTS IN THE TREBLE, BASS AND ALTO CLEFS

A. C Flute, Oboe, C Trumpet (orch.) Violin, Tubular Chimes (Tubular Bells)

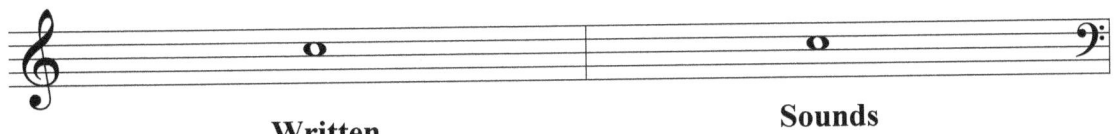

Written   Sounds

B. Bassoon, Tenor Trombone, Bass Trombone, Baritone (Euphonium) Tuba, Violoncello (Cello), Timpani

Written   Sounds

C. Viola

Written   Sounds

2. INSTRUMENTS IN THE TREBLE CLEF SOUNDING ONE OCTAVE HIGHER THAN WRITTEN

A. C Piccolo, Xylohone

Written   Sounds

3. INSTRUMENTS WRITTEN IN THE TREBLE CLEF SOUNDING ONE OCTAVE LOWER THAN WRITTEN

A. Guitar

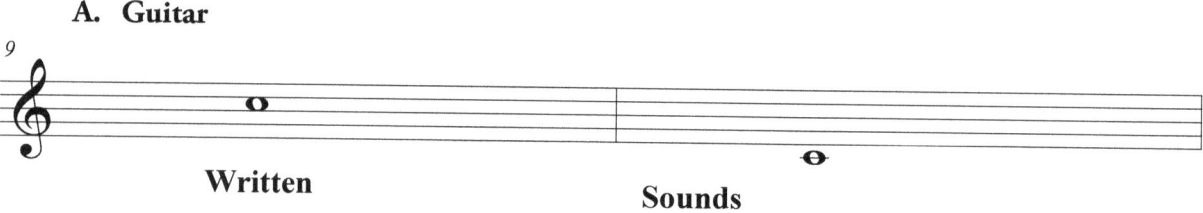

4. INSTRUMENTS USING THE GRAND STAFF (TREBLE & BASS CLEFS)

A. Piano, Organ, Synthesizer, Marimba, Harp, Roto-toms, Vibraphone

B. Celesta

C. Glockenspiel (Orchestra Bells) (Bell Lyre)

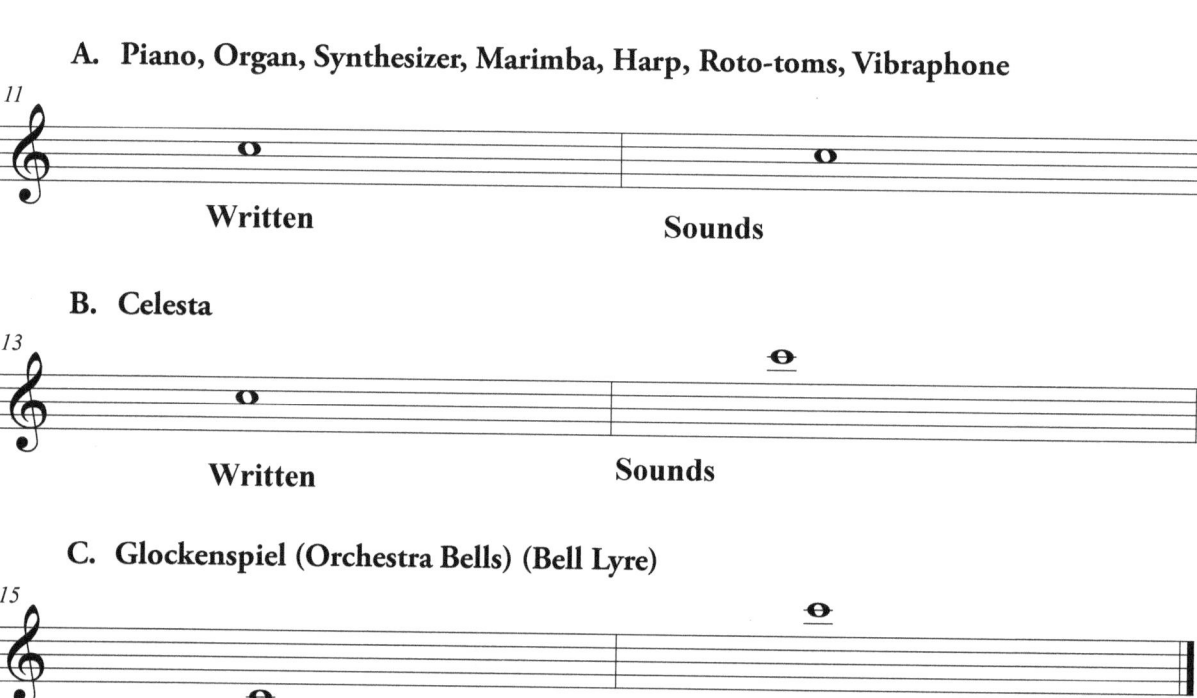

5. *INSTRUMENTS WRITTEN IN THE BASS CLEF SOUNDING ONE OCTAVE LOWER THAN WRITTEN*

A. Contrabass (String Bass) Bass Guitar

Written   Sounds

6. *INSTRUMENTS WRITTEN IN THE TREBLE CLEF SOUNDING A MINOR 3rd HIGHER THAN WRITTEN*

A. Eb Clarinet, Eb Cornet

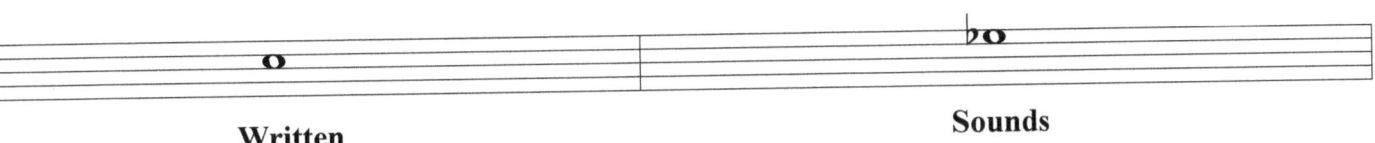

Written   Sounds

7. *INSTRUMENTS SOUNDING A WHOLE TONE (MAJOR 2nd) LOWER THAN WRITTEN*

A. Bb Trumpet, Bb Cornet, Bb Clarinet, Bb Soprano Sax

Written   Sounds

8. *Bb INSTRUMENTS SOUNDING AN OCTAVE AND A WHOLE TONE (MAJOR 9th) LOWER THAN WRITTEN*

A. Bb Bass Clarinet, Bb Tenor Saxophone

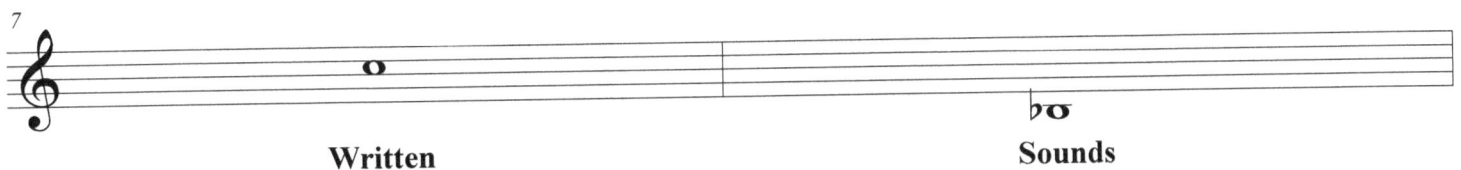

Written   Sounds

9. INSTRUMENTS SOUNDING A PERFECT 5th LOWER THAN WRITTEN

A. F French Horn

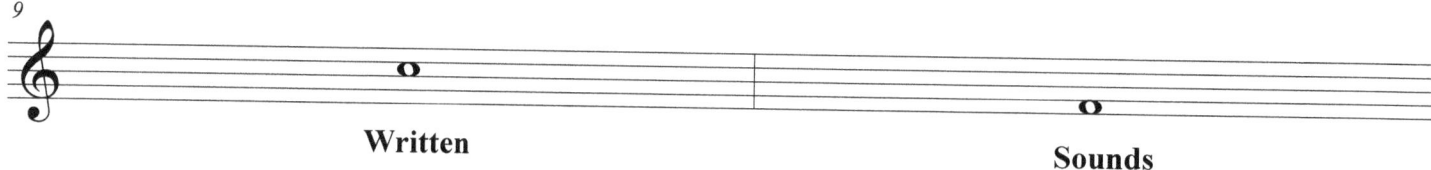

Written   Sounds

10. Eb INSTRUMENTS SOUNDING A MAJOR 6th LOWER THAN WRITTEN

A. Eb Alto Clarinet, Eb Alto Saxophone

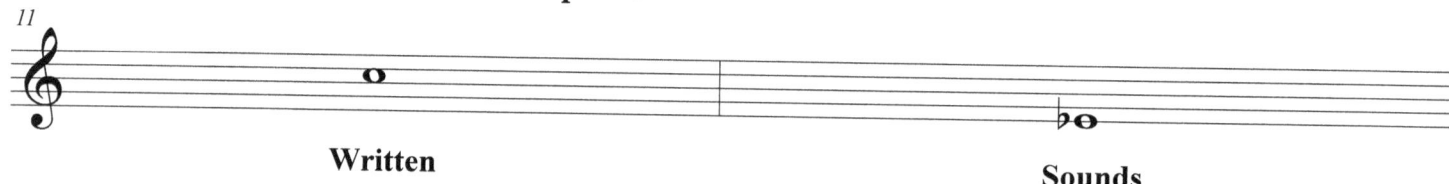

Written   Sounds

11. Eb INSTRUMENTS SOUNDING ONE OCTAVE + A MAJOR 6th (MAJOR 13th) LOWER THAN WRITTEN

A. Eb Baritone Saxophone

Written   Sounds

WRITING FOR INSTRUMENTS

1. **Write the following instruments at concert pitch:**

(Treble Clef)	C Flute, Oboe, Violin, Tubular Chimes, Vibraphone, C Trumpet (orchestra)
(Alto Clef)	Viola
(Bass Clef)	Bassoon, Tenor & Bass Trombones, Baritone (Euphonium Bass Clef), Tuba, Cello, Timpani

2. **Write the following instruments at concert pitch using the Grand Staff:**

   Piano, Harp, Organ, Synthesizer, Marimba, Roto-Toms

3. **Write the following instruments one octave lower than concert pitch:**

   C Piccolo, Xylophone, Celesta

4. **Write the following instruments two octaves lower than concert pitch:**

   Glockenspiel (Orchestra Bells)

5. **Write the following instruments one octave higher than concert pitch:**

   Guitar, Contrabass (String Bass), Bass Guitar

6. **Write the following instruments one tone (major 2nd) higher than concert pitch:**

   Bb Trumpet, Bb Cornet, Bb Clarinet, Bb Soprano Saxophone

7. **Write the following instruments one octave + one tone (major 9th) higher than concert pitch:**

   Bb Bass Clarinet, Bb Tenor Saxophone, Baritone (Euphonium Treble Clef)

8. **Write the following instrument a perfect 5th higher than concert pitch:**

   F French Horn

9. **Write the following instrument a minor 3rd lower than concert pitch:**

   Eb Clarinet, Eb Cornet

10. **Write the following instruments a major 6th higher than the concert pitch:**

    Eb Alto Clarinet, Eb Alto Saxophone

11. **Write the following instrument a Major 6th + one octave (major 13th_ higher than the concert pitch:**

    Eb Baritone Saxophone

WRITING KEY SIGNATURES

1. All *non-transposing instruments* in the treble, alto, and bass clefs and those that transpose up or down one or two octaves play in the *concert key*.

2. All *F transposing instruments* play with a key signature that has *one sharp more* or *one flat less* than the concert key.

3. All *Bb transposing instruments* play with a key signature that has *two sharps more* or *two flats less* than the concert key.

4. All *Eb transposing instruments* play with a key signature that has *three sharps more* or *three flats less* than the concert key.

EXAMPLES:

Concert Key	Non-transposing	F Inst.	Bb Inst.	Eb Inst.
G(e)	G(e)	D(b)	A(f#)	E(c#)
Ab(f)	Ab(f)	Eb(c)	Bb(g)	F(d)
F(d)*	F(d)	C(a)	G(e)	D(b)

*(Note: In this case, there is only one flat in the concert key. Therefore, you subtract one flat add one sharp for Bb instruments, and you subtract one flat and add two sharps for Eb instruments)

Assignment #1

For each of the measures below, write the actual concert pitch sound . You may find that some instruments, although written in the treble clef, actually sound in the bass clef. Use accidentals rather than key signatures. Make sure you write the clef and time signature.

WRITTEN RANGES OF INSTRUMENTS

(Note: The ranges listed below are realistic ranges for the average high school senior student. It should be realized that the possible ranges for beginning and junior band students and for professional musicians will be significantly different in some cases.)

THE WOODWINDS

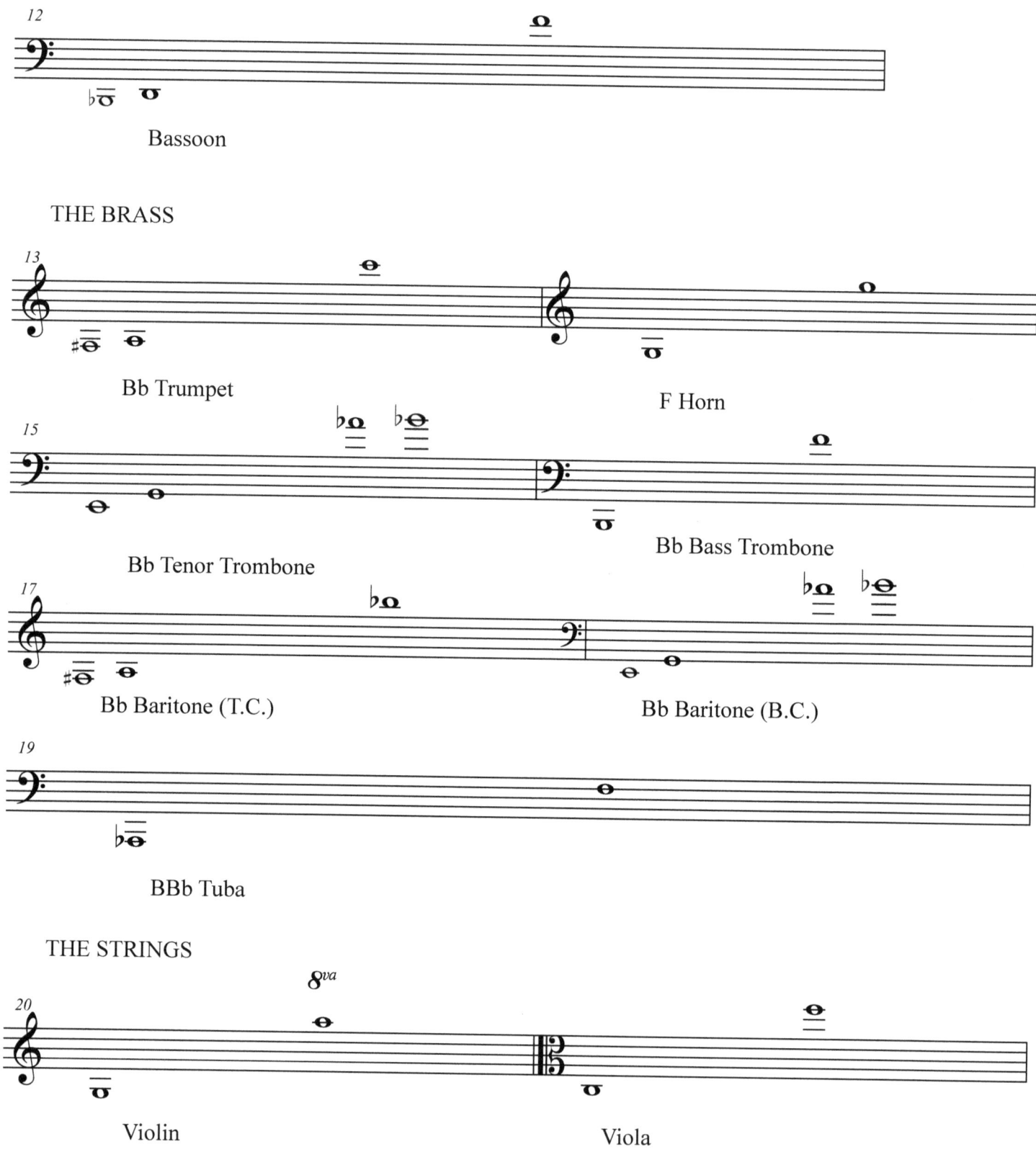

Bassoon

THE BRASS

Bb Trumpet

F Horn

Bb Tenor Trombone

Bb Bass Trombone

Bb Baritone (T.C.)

Bb Baritone (B.C.)

BBb Tuba

THE STRINGS

Violin

Viola

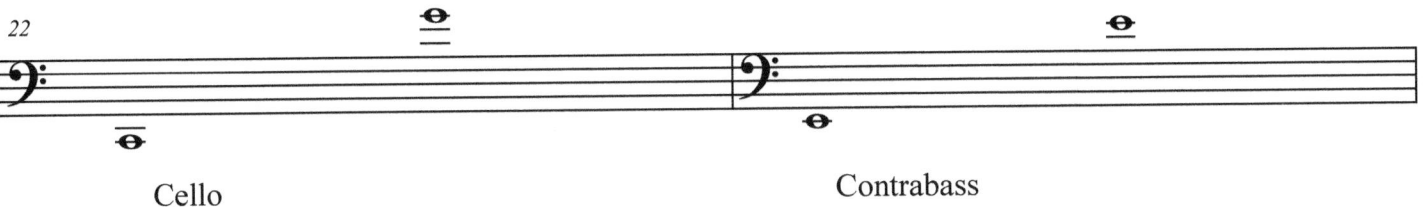

Cello   Contrabass

THE PERCUSSION

Timpani   30"   28"   25"   23"

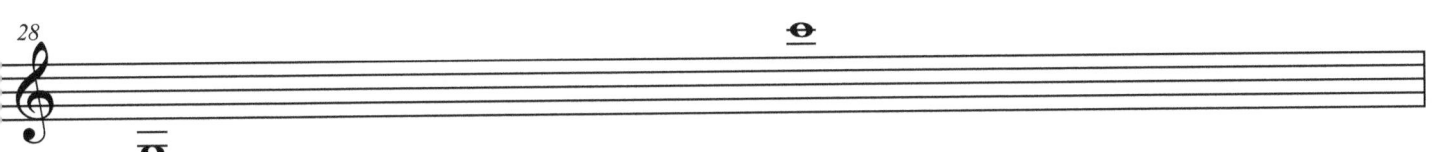

Orchestra Bells (Glockenspiel)

Xylophone   *8va*   Tubular Bells (Chimes)

Marimba   Vibraphone

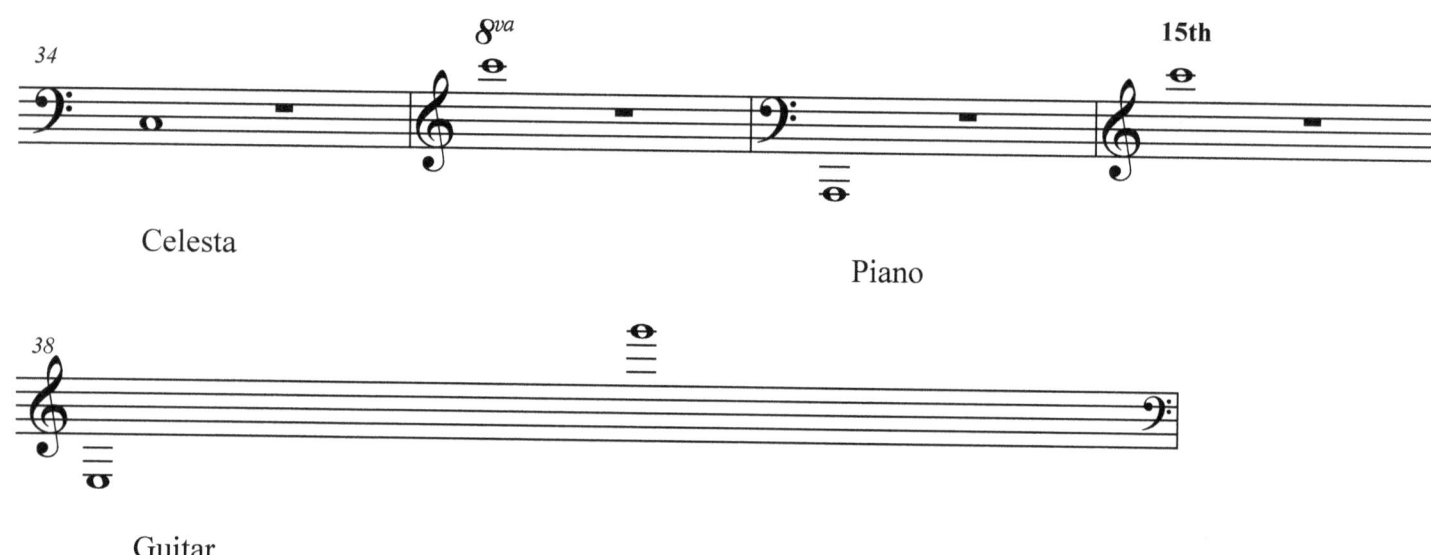

Celesta

Piano

Guitar

Roto-toms (various sizes)

Diameter

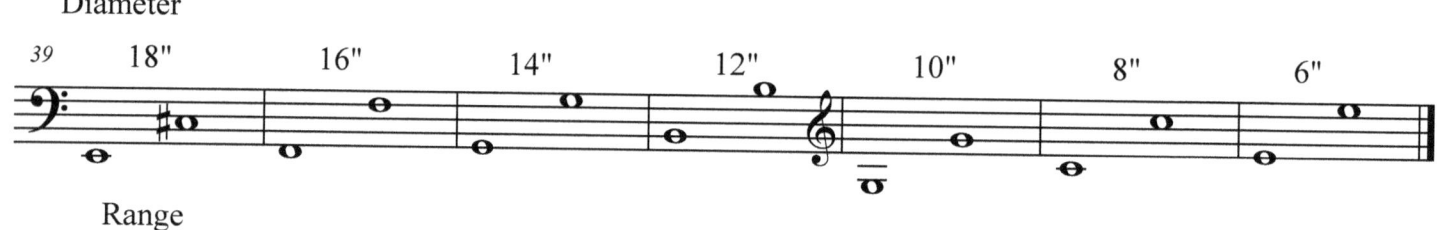

Range

Assignment #2

Practice with Instrument Ranges
For each of the instruments listed below, write the written range

Assignment #3

PRELIMINARY EXERCISES IN OCTAVE TRANSPOSITION

1. Write the following melody one octave higher in the Treble Clef

2. Write the following melody one octave higher in the bass clef.

3. Write the following melody one octave higher in the Treble Clef:

4. Write the following melody two octaves higher in the Treble Clef:

14

WORKING WITH INTERVALS
(A Review of Rudiments)

1. Intervals are shown by number. They include: Unisons, 2nds, 3rds, 4ths, 5ths, 6ths, 6ths, Octaves, 9ths, 10ths, 11ths, 12ths, 13ths. Examples of intervals are included below:

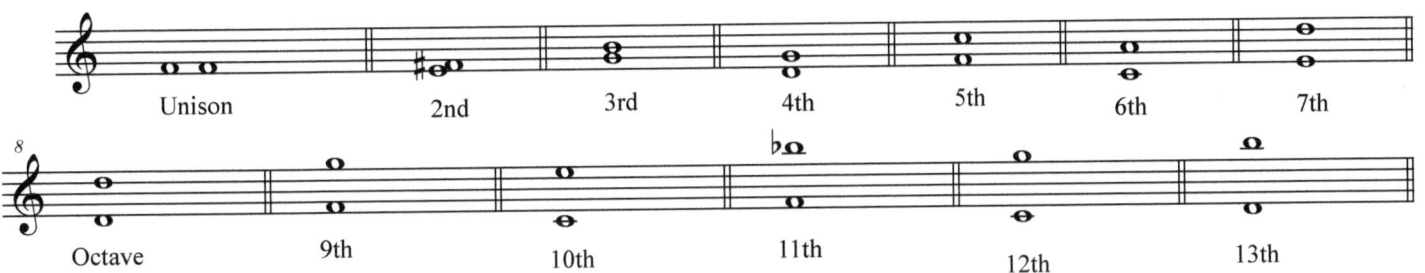

2. Intervals are of different types. Types of intervals are: Major (+), Minor (-), Diminished (o), Augmented (X), and Perfect (P). Some examples of each type of interval are shown below.

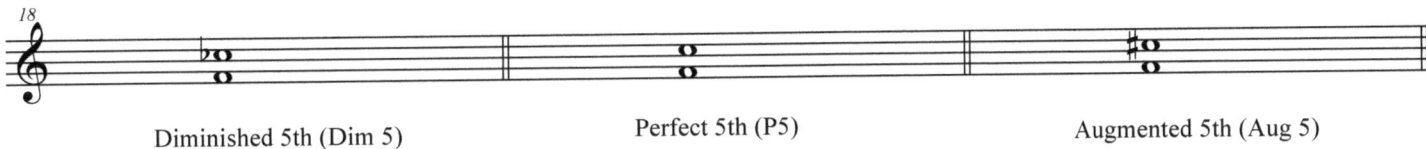

3. Unisons, Octaves, 4ths, 5ths, 11ths, and 12ths can be Perfect, Augmented, or Diminished. Examples of these intervals are shown below:

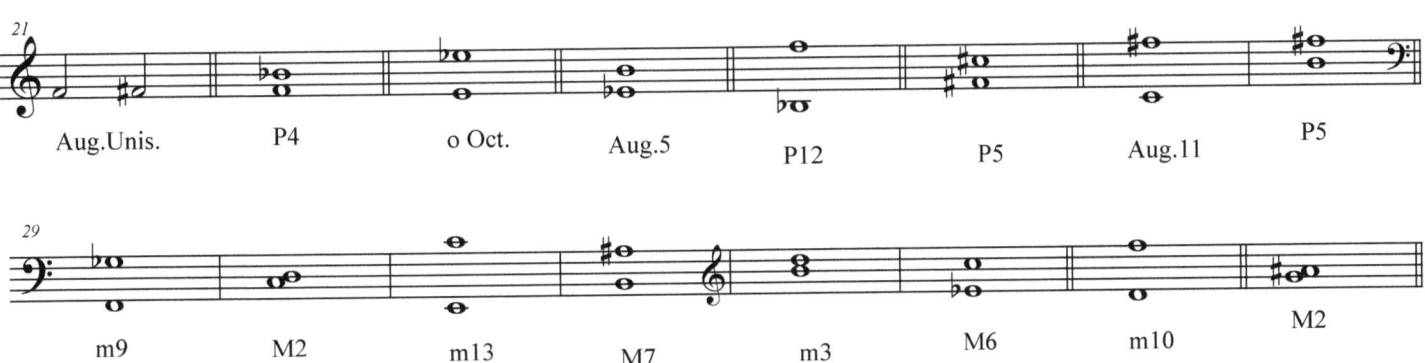

Assignment #4

PRACTICE WRITING INTERVALS

Write the following intervals as indicated below:

m6   M7   Aug. 11   o5   P5   M9   m2   POct

Write the following intervals above the given notes;

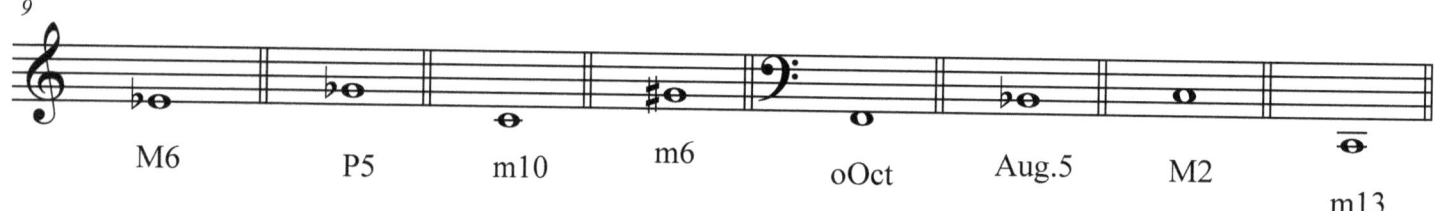

M6   P5   m10   m6   oOct   Aug.5   M2   m13

Write the following intervals below the given notes:

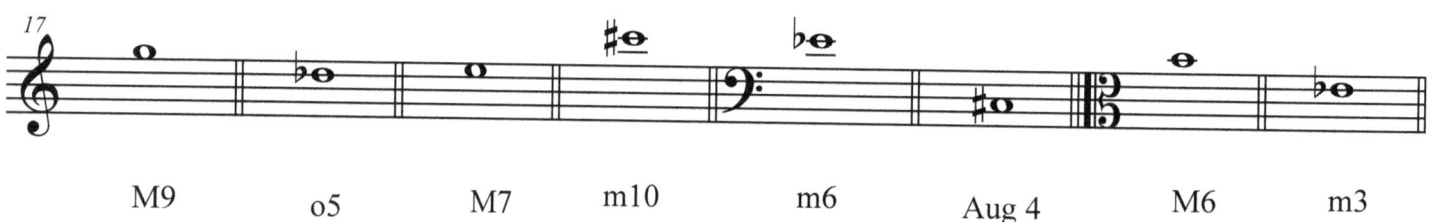

M9   o5   M7   m10   m6   Aug 4   M6   m3

PRELIMINARY EXERCISES IN TRANSPOSITION

Assignment #5

Write the following melody (concert pitch) for the instruments listed below. Make sure you change the key signature if necessary and raise or lower each note the correct interval. You may have to change the direction of the stems. Be neat! (Hint: Draw barlines of the transposed parts directly below the barlines of the original melody).

C Flute (one octave higher)

Bb Clarinet

Eb Alto Sax

F Horn

Guitar

Trombone (one octave lower)

WHAT TO DO ABOUT ACCIDENTALS

When transposing an original melody in concert pitch for transposing instruments, you must follow certain steps. There are two methods you might try.

Method #1: Look at the key signature of the original. Look at the note(s) with accidentals. If the note is raised a semitone in the original, for example, Bb was raised to a B-natural, then the note in the transposed part must be raised a semitone. An example of this is indicated below.

Notice that in the original, the F was raised to F# in measure 1, the G is raised to a G# in measure 2. Therefore, in the transposed Bb Trumpet part, the G is raised to a G#, and the A is raised to an A#. Similarly, in measures 3 and 4, the B was lowered to a Bb, the A was lowered to an Ab, and the D was lowered to a Db. Therefore, in the transposed Bb Trumpet part, the C# was lowered to a C-natural, the B was lowered to a Bb, and the E was lowered to an Eb.

Method #2 (using the same example): For transposing a concert pitch part for Bb Trumpet, one must write the transposed part 1 tone (or 2 semitones) higher than the concert pitch. Look at each accidental in the original, and then raise it by 1 tone. Therefore, the F# becomes a G#, G# becomes A#, Bb becomes C, Ab becomes Bb, and Db becomes Eb.

Note: Any note which contains an accidental in the concert pitch melody MUST have an accidental in the transposed part.

PRACTISE TRANSPOSING A MELODY WITH ACCIDENTALS

Assignment #6

Write the following melody (concert pitch) for the instruments listed below. Use the correct key signature for each instrument. Make sure you raise or lower each note the correct interval. Remember: Every accidental in the original melody will have an accidental in the transposed part. You may have to change the direction of the stems. Hint: Draw the barlines of the transposed parts directly below the barlines of the original melody.)

C Flute (one octave higher)

Bb Clarinet

Eb Alto Sax

F Horn

Marimba

Tuba (two octaves lower)

Assignment #7

Transpose the concert pitch melody below for the instruments listed. Make sure you:
i. Use the correct clef
ii. Write the correct key ignature
iii. Write the time signature
iv. Transpose up or down the correct interval
v. Treat the accidentals properly
vi. Add the dynamic markings
vii. Add the proper phrase markings
viii. Add the crescendos and diminuendos

Assignment #8

Arrange the following two-measure chorale phrase for the instruments listed below. Make sure you use the correct clef, key signature, and time signature and transpose each instrument properly. Watch the fermata at the end.

Assignment #9

TRANSPOSITION PRACTICE

Transpose the following piece up a minor third. Make sure you change all of the accidentals

Assignment #10

First, transpose the following excerpt into the key of Eb:

Key of Eb

Assignment #11

Now transcribe the ercerpt for woodwind quintet (flute, oboe, Bb clarinet, F horn, and bassoon).

Suggestion: Give the melody to the oboe and then double it an octave higher for the flute. Make sure you label each part, choose the correct clef for each instrument, choose the correct key signature for each instrument, write the time signature in each part, change the stem directions if necessary, make sure each beat in the bar is aligned vertically, add the dynamic marking to each part, and make sure that the fermatas are added to each part and placed above each part.

Assignment #12

Arrange the following Chorale tune by J. S. Bach for brass quintet (2 Bb trumpets, F Horn, Trombone, and Tuba). Make sure you have the correct key signature for each instrument and you transpose each part the correct interval.

Note: Write the tuba part one octave lower than the bass part of the original. Be neat! Rule all barlines. Use the correct space for each measure. Make sure the stem directions are correct. Make sure each beat in the measure is vertically-spaced correctly

* Chorale tune from J. S. Bach's Cantata No. 78, "Jesu, der du meine Seele"

2

Assignment #13

Arrange the following piece for string quartet (2 violins, viola, and cello).

Violin 1

Violin 2

Viola

Cello

5

Vl1

5

Vl2

5

Vla

5

Vcl

9

Vl1

9

Vl2

9

Vla

9

Vcl

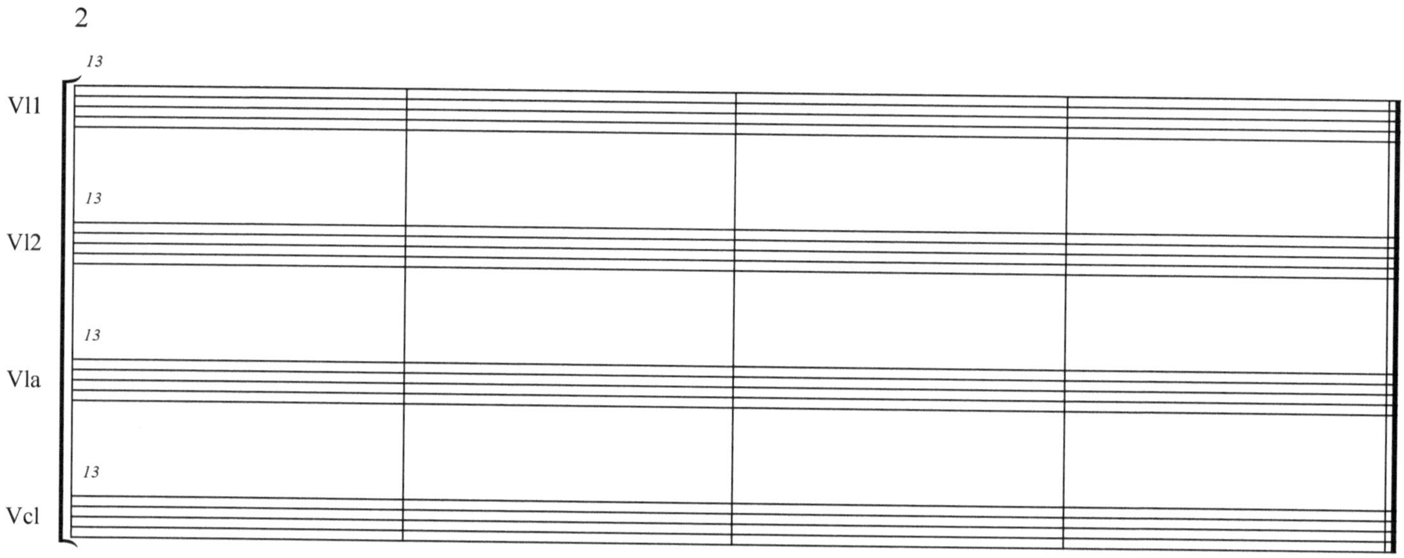

2

13

Vl1

13

Vl2

13

Vla

13

Vcl

Assignment #14

Arrange the following piece for any combination of four instruments found in your instrumental class. Make sure the range of the instrument is suitable and that each of the instruments blends well together. Add a suitable tempo marking, dynamics, and phrase markings to your arrangement. Perform the piece for your classmates.

5

5

5

5

Scoring for Percussion

In concert band scores, the percussion is placed at the bottom of the score. In orchestra scores, it is placed between the winds (woodwinds and brass) and the strings. Generally the timpani is placed on the top line of the percussion section, followed by the mallet instruments, then the unpitched percussion including snare drum and bass drum, triangle, tambourine, cymbals, etc.

There are many different ways of notating percussion. Look at the examples below to get an idea of some of the more common methods.

i. Timpani and mallet instruments usually use the five-line staff.

ii. Sometimes the snare and bass drums are notated on the five-line staff as in

Example 1 (the snare on the third space, the bass on the first space); sometimes they are on the one-line staff as in Example 2 (the snare drum above the line, the bass below).

iii. Sometimes all of the non-pitched percussion instruments are placed on their own single-line staff as in Example 3.

Example 1

Example 2

Example 3

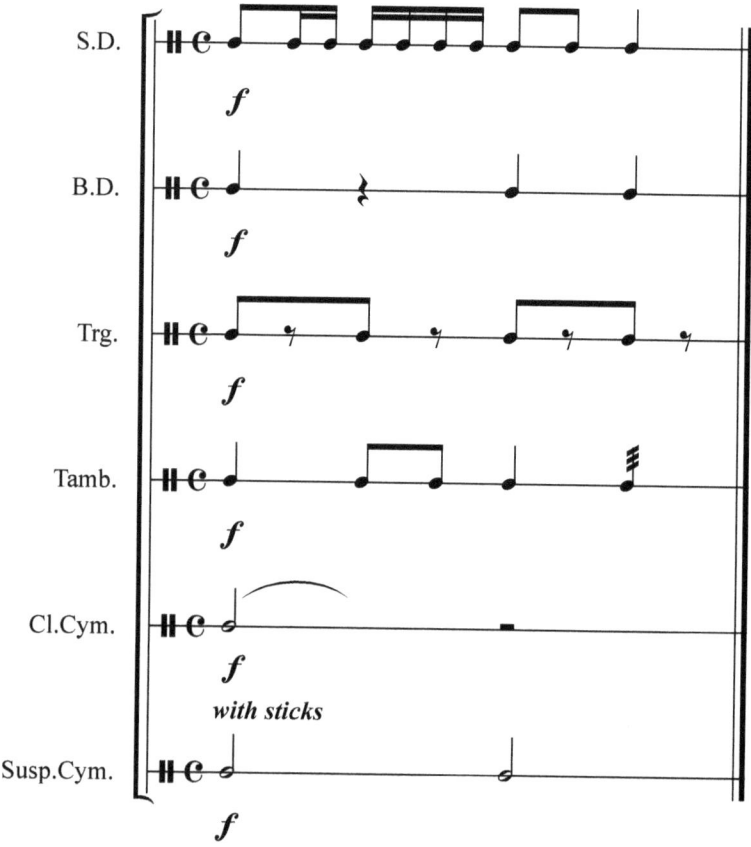

Some Suggestions for Transcribing a Bach Chorale Tune for Concert Band

Note: For your first concert band score, it is suggested that you stick to the suggestions which follow. After you have some experience with transcribing a basic Bach chorale for band, then you can begin experimenting with more creative instrumental combinations and scoring techniques. But this is a topic for Volume 2. Also in Volume 2, percussion techniques will be discussed and illustrated in more detail. For now, if you think of each section woodwinds and brass as SATB arrangements in themselves, the resulting sound will be at least balanced and full.

As the number of parts increases, you will need larger paper to write your arrangements. This paper is available from your local music store, or you can make your own paper. There are also many music copying programs available for your computer such as Sibelius and Finale. Your music teacher will be able to suggest a program to fit your needs. Perhaps your music department has programs at the school that you can use.

The following are some suggestions you might use in transcribing a chorale tune for band:

1. The flute plays the melody line one octave higher.

2. Oboes play the melody or a harmony part, probably the alto line. The oboe sounds best in its middle register.

3. The first clarinet plays the melody while the second and third clarinets play harmony parts below.

4. The alto clarinet doubles the bass line or an inner harmony part.

5. The bassoon can play the bass line or a lower inner part.

6. The bass clarinet plays the bass part.

7. The saxophones fill in between the clarinets and lower woodwinds. The baritone sax plays the bass line.

8. The first trumpet plays the melody while the second and third trumpets play harmony parts.

9. Horns fill in between the trumpet and trombone parts.

10. Trombones play harmony parts in the lower register.

11. The baritone doubles the bass line or a moving lower inner part.

12. The tuba plays the bass line.

13. The percussion act as embellishment much the same as spice is added to food. Mallet instruments can reinforce melody or harmony parts. The timpani can reinforce the basic harmony especially at cadence points. Other percussion instruments can be added to taste.

Assignment #15

Arrange the following Bach chorale tune for concert band. Read the general principles of writing for concert band found on page 35

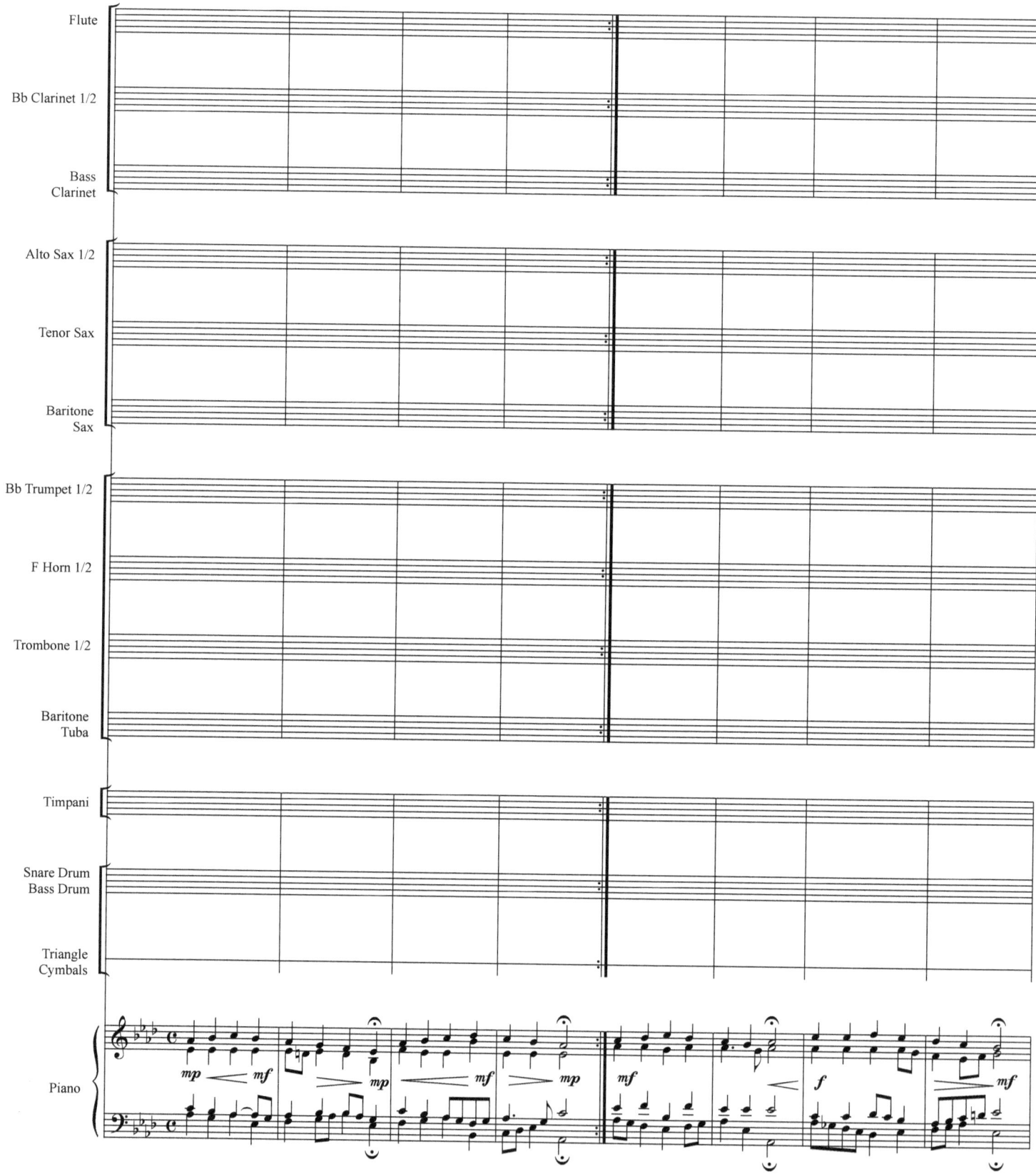

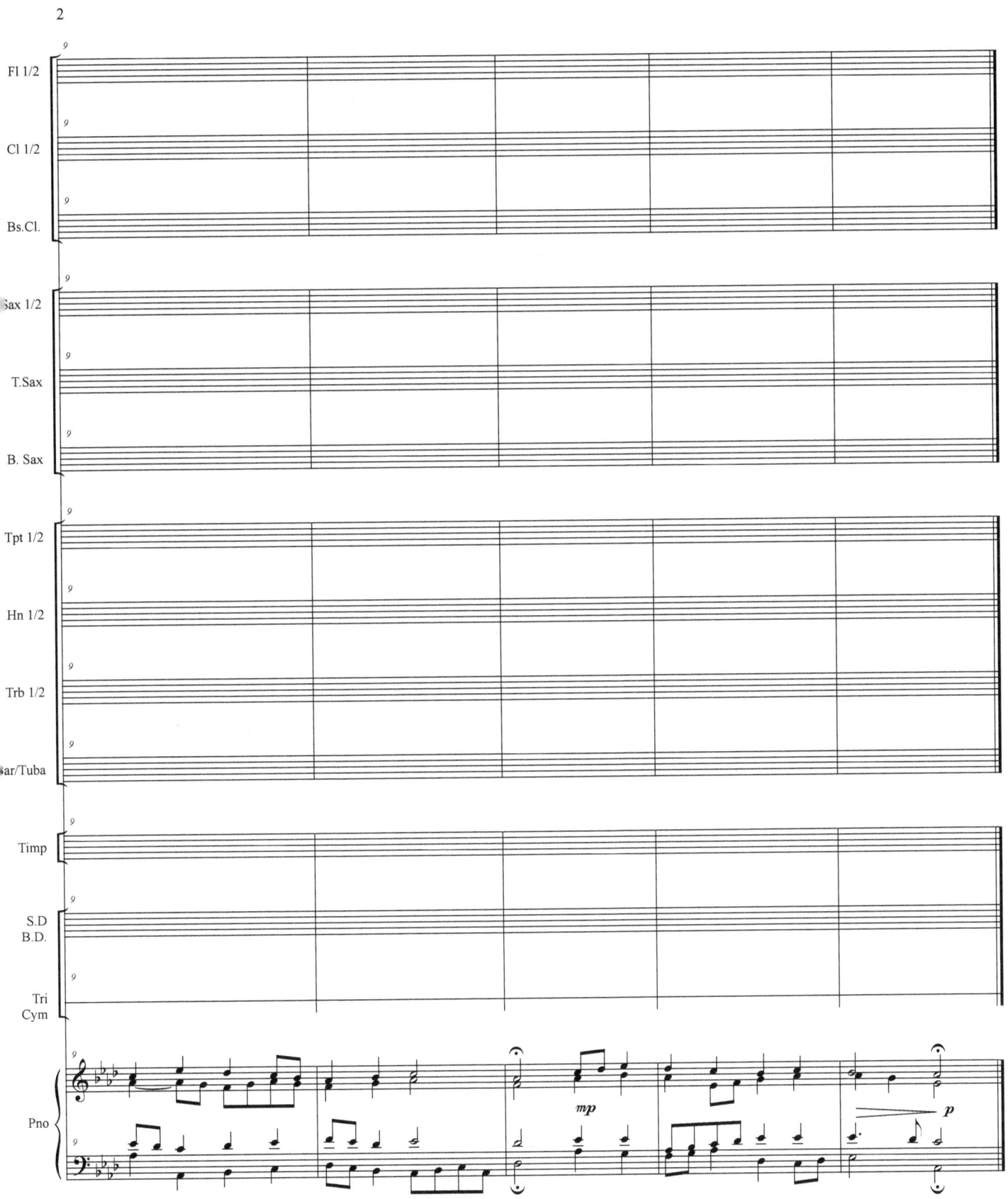

General Considerations for Arranging

The following should be added to each score:

1. Title

2. Composer

3. Arranger

4. Tempo marking; e.g., Allegro, Andante, Slowly, Majestically, etc.

5. Metronome marking e.g. quarter note = 60

6. Label every staff (left margin of the score). The first page of the score contains all the instruments used in the piece in long form; the second and following pages show each instrument in short form. Of course, all instruments should be in proper score order.

7. Dynamic markings under each individual part, including crescendos and diminuendos

8. Articulations such as staccato, tenuto, accents, fermatas, etc.

9. Phrase and slur markings in all parts; bowings indicated in any string parts

10. Stem directions are correct. If there are two parts on the same staff, make sure the upper part stems go up, the lower part stems go down..

11. General tempo indications pertaining to all instruments such as rit., a tempo, slowly, etc. above top line of the score and above the trumpets (cornets)

12. Some sort of numbering of the measures: every 5 measures, letters at the beginning of important places in the score, every measure numbered, etc.

13. Correct Clef for each instrument

14. Time signature at beginning and all changes of time signatures throughout the score

15. Key signatures for each instrument line and changes in key throughout

16. Barlines drawn as vertical lines joining all instruments of a section

17. Score aligned vertically, each beat and subdivision of each beat aligned

18. Make sure all percussion instruments are labeled properly. Add indications about the type of mallet or stick to use.

19. Pages should be numbered.

20. A copyright notice can be put at the bottom of the first page of score;

21. e.g., Copyright © 2003, DWR MUSIC. All rights reserved.

List of Materials Used in Assignments

1. **Joy to the World** - Christmas Carol - melody adapted by Lowell Mason (1792 - 1872), pg.14

2. **Promenade** from **"Pictures at an Exhibition"** by Modest Mussorgsky (1839 - 81), pg. 14

3. **"Every Valley"** from **Messiah** by Georges Frederick Handel (1685 - 1759)

4. **"Carefree"** from **"Autumn in Retrospect"** (mov't 2) by Dr. David W. Roe, pg. 14

5. **O Canada** by Calixa Lavallee (1842 - 91), pg. 17

6. **Music for Brass Quintet** (mov't 1) by Dr. David W. Roe, pg.19

7. **"Freundlich sehr, o meine Seele"** from **371 4-part Chorales** by J.S. Bach (1685 - 1750), pg. 21

8. **The Coventry Carol**, traditional, pg. 22

9. **O Sacred Head Sore Wounded** by Hans Hassler (1564 - 1612), harmonization by J.S. Bach (1685 - 1750), pg. 23

10. **"Jesu, der meine Seele"** from **Cantata No. 78,** by J.S. Bach, pg. 25

11. **"Morgenbet" (Morning Prayer)** from **The Album for the Young** by Peter Ilyich Tchaikovsky (1840 - 93), pg. 28

12. **By the Cradle**, Op.68, no.5 by Edvard Grieg, pg. 31

13. **"Freu' dich sehr, o meine Seele"** from **371 4-part Chorales** by J.S. Bach (1685 - 1750), pg. 36-37

BIBLIOGRAPHY
Suggestions for Further study

Adler, Samuel. **The Study of Orchestration**, 2nd ed. New York: W.W. Norton & Company, Inc., 1989.

Andrews, William G. and Molly Sclater. **Materials of Western Music**, Part 1. Toronto, Canada: Gordon V. Thompson Music, 1987.

Blatter, Alfred. **Instrumentation/Orchestration**. New York: Longman Inc., 1980.

Cacavas, John. **Music Arranging and Orchestration**. Melville, N.Y.: Belwin-Mills Publishing Corp., 1975.

Delamont, Gordon. **Modern Arranging Technique**. Delevan, N.Y.: Kendor Music, Inc., 1965.

Donato, Anthony. **Preparing Music Manuscript**. Englewood Cliffs, New Jersey: Prentice-Hall, Inc., 1963.

Erickson, Frank. **Arranging for the Concert Band**. Melville, N.Y.: Belwin- Mills Publishing Corp., 1983.

Reed, Gardner. **Music Notation: A Manual of Modern Practice**, 2nd ed. New York: Taplinger Publishing Company, 1979.

Reed, H.Owen and Joel T. Leach. **Scoring for Percussion**. Melville, N.Y.: Belwin-Mills Publishing Corp., 1969.

Sarnecki, Mark. **Harmony**, Book One. Mississauga, Ontario, Canada: The Frederick Harris Music Co., Ltd., 2000.

Wharram, Barbara. **Elementary Rudiments of Music**. Mississauga, Ontario, Canada: The Frederick Harris Music Co., Ltd., 1969.

ABOUT THE AUTHOR

Dr. David W. Roe is a teacher, composer, arranger, conductor and trombonist. For many years, he has been a teacher of instrumental and vocal music in the secondary schools of Ontario, Canada.

Dr. Roe began his post secondary studies at the University of Toronto where he graduated with a Mus. Bac. Degree in Music Education. At the same time, he received the A.R.C.T. Diploma in Trombone from the Royal Conservatory. The year after graduating, he had the opportunity of studying at the Akademie fur Music und darstellende Kunst in Vienna, Austria. Later in his teaching career, he returned to graduate school at the University of Miami, Florida, where he earned the Master of Music and Doctor of Musical Arts Degrees in Music Composition.

Dr. Roe has written many compositions for symphony orchestra, concert band, woodwind, brass, string and percussion ensembles, choir and organ, and English handbells. His compositions have been performed in Canada and the United States.

www.ingramcontent.com/pod-product-compliance
Lightning Source LLC
Chambersburg PA
CBHW041127120626
46547CB00019B/2881